I0117089

Renewing the Atlantic Partnership

Report of an Independent Task Force
Sponsored by the
Council on Foreign Relations

Henry A. Kissinger and Lawrence H. Summers,
Co-Chairs
Charles A. Kupchan, Project Director

Founded in 1921, the Council on Foreign Relations is an independent, national member-ship organization and a nonpartisan center for scholars dedicated to producing and dis-seminating ideas so that individual and corporate members, as well as policymakers, journalists, students, and interested citizens in the United States and other countries, can better understand the world and the foreign policy choices facing the United States and other governments. The Council does this by convening meetings; conducting a wide-ranging Studies program; publishing *Foreign Affairs*, the preeminent journal covering inter-national affairs and U.S. foreign policy; maintaining a diverse membership; sponsoring Independent Task Forces; and providing up-to-date information about the world and U.S. foreign policy on the Council's website, www.cfr.org.

THE COUNCIL TAKES NO INSTITUTIONAL POSITION ON POLICY ISSUES AND HAS NO AFFILIATION WITH THE U.S. GOVERNMENT. ALL STATE-MENTS OF FACT AND EXPRESSIONS OF OPINION CONTAINED IN ITS PUB-LICATIONS ARE THE SOLE RESPONSIBILITY OF THE AUTHOR OR AUTHORS.

The Council will sponsor an Independent Task Force when (1) an issue of current and critical importance to U.S. foreign policy arises, and (2) it seems that a group diverse in backgrounds and perspectives may, nonetheless, be able to reach a meaningful consensus on a policy through private and nonpartisan deliberations. Typically, a Task Force meets between two and five times over a brief period to ensure the relevance of its work.

Upon reaching a conclusion, a Task Force issues a report, and the Council publishes its text and posts it on the Council website. Task Force reports can take three forms: (1) a strong and meaningful policy consensus, with Task Force members endorsing the general policy thrust and judgments reached by the group, though not necessarily every finding and rec-ommendation; (2) a report stating the various policy positions, each as sharply and fairly as possible; or (3) a "Chairman's Report," where Task Force members who agree with the chairman's report may associate themselves with it, while those who disagree may submit dissenting statements. Upon reaching a conclusion, a Task Force may also ask individuals who were not members of the Task Force to associate themselves with the Task Force report to enhance its impact. All Task Force reports "benchmark" their findings against current administration policy in order to make explicit areas of agreement and disagreement. The Task Force is solely responsible for its report. The Council takes no institutional position.

For further information about the Council or this Task Force, please write to the Council on Foreign Relations, 58 East 68th Street, New York, NY 10021, or call the Direc-tor of Communications at 212-434-9400. Visit the Council's website at www.cfr.org.

Copyright © 2004 by the Council on Foreign Relations®, Inc.

All rights reserved.

Printed in the United States of America.

This report may not be reproduced in whole or in part, in any form beyond the reproduc-tion permitted by Sections 107 and 108 of the U.S. Copyright Law Act (17 U.S.C. Sections 107 and 108) and excerpts by reviewers for the public press, without express written per-mission from the Council on Foreign Relations. For information, write to the Publications Office, Council on Foreign Relations, 58 East 68th Street, New York, NY 10021.

TASK FORCE MEMBERS

Giuliano Amato

Reginald Bartholomew

Douglas K. Bereuter

Harold Brown

Richard R. Burt

Thierry de Montbrial

Thomas E. Donilon

Stuart E. Eizenstat

Martin Feldstein

John Lewis Gaddis

Timothy Garton Ash

G. John Ikenberry

Josef Joffe

Robert Kagan

Henry A. Kissinger
Co-Chair

Charles A. Kupchan
Project Director

Sylvia Mathews

Andrew Moravcsik

Andrzej Olechowski

Felix G. Rohatyn

Brent Scowcroft

Anne-Marie Slaughter

Lawrence H. Summers
Co-Chair

Daniel K. Tarullo

Laura D'Andrea Tyson

Stephen M. Walt*

*The individual has endorsed the report and submitted an additional view.

CONTENTS

FOREWORD

The Atlantic alliance has been a critical component of the international system for the last five decades. Through joint efforts to pursue shared interests, the United States and its European allies succeeded not just in containing the Soviet threat (and in fostering conditions that contributed to the ultimate demise of the Soviet Union itself) but also in liberalizing the global economy and extending democratic governance to Europe's east and beyond.

The transatlantic relationship is now under serious strain. The end of the Cold War, Europe's continuing integration, and the new array of threats confronting the West have led Americans and Europeans alike to question the durability and utility of the Atlantic alliance. The transatlantic rift that opened over the war in Iraq significantly intensified these concerns.

The Council on Foreign Relations established this independent, bipartisan Task Force to examine how to revitalize the Atlantic alliance. The Cold War is over, but cooperation across the Atlantic will remain critical for addressing the regional and increasingly global challenges likely to be central in the twenty-first century.

The Task Force, consisting of both Americans and Europeans, argues that despite the forces pushing apart the two sides of the Atlantic, the United States and Europe still have compatible interests and complementary capabilities. The Task Force makes a strong case that the United States and Europe should reassess existing principles governing the use of military force and seek to reach agreement on new "rules of the road." Similarly, it argues that America and Europe should develop a common policy toward states that possess or seek to possess weapons of mass destruction or that support terrorism in any way.

Task Force recommendations also address the future of NATO, the need for Americans and Europeans to work in tandem to promote political and economic reform in the greater Middle East, and the desirability of expanding development and trade. A central theme of the report is the importance of increasing the frequency and improving the quality of transatlantic consultations. America may be the indispensable nation, but its partners in Europe are its indispensable allies. Virtually every objective that Americans and Europeans seek will be easier to attain if they work together—but this is something that will happen only if the transatlantic dialogue is frank, timely, and judicious.

The Council is deeply grateful that two distinguished American statesmen were willing to dedicate time and energy to this effort: Dr. Henry A. Kissinger, the former secretary of state and national security adviser and current chairman of Kissinger Associates, Inc.; and Dr. Lawrence H. Summers, the former secretary of the treasury and current president of Harvard University. Henry and Larry did an excellent job of chairing the Task Force. Charles A. Kupchan, senior fellow at the Council and our director of Europe studies, directed the project from inception to the final edits on this report. My heartfelt thanks to Henry, Larry, and Charlie for their hard work.

I would also like to thank Eni, Fundación Juan March, Fondation pour la Science et la Culture, Merrill Lynch, and the German Marshall Fund of the United States for their generous financial support of the Task Force.

This report not only helps to explain the recent past but presents a forward-looking agenda for making the transatlantic relationship more robust and more relevant. These are objectives that should appeal to both Americans and Europeans. I am confident that the work of this Task Force will make a significant contribution to the transatlantic dialogue and provide leaders and citizens on both sides of the Atlantic with the logic and a path for future cooperation.

Richard N. Haass
President
Council on Foreign Relations
March 2004

[viii]

ACKNOWLEDGMENTS

We could not have asked for a more able and distinguished group of individuals to join us in deliberating about the future of the Atlantic alliance. We would like to extend our gratitude to the members of the Task Force for the time and intellectual energy they devoted to our effort. Special thanks are due John Lewis Gaddis, Andrew Moravcsik, and Stephen M. Walt, all of whom lent a hand in drafting this report. In addition, Charles Hill provided wise outside counsel as the draft report was taking shape. We are also grateful to Gordon Brown, Wolfgang Ischinger, Jean-David Levitte, and Karsten Voigt for meeting with the Task Force; their views provided valuable input.

The Task Force benefited from excellent staff support. Jamie Fly at the Council did a remarkable job as the overall coordinator of our efforts. We were fortunate to have the services of two of the Council's military fellows, Colonel Walter Givhan and Colonel Peter Henry, each of whom made important contributions to the Task Force. Leah Pisar served as a dedicated rapporteur at each of the Task Force's meetings. Lee Feinstein, the deputy director of studies and executive director of task forces, was a steady source of guidance. Patricia Dorff, Lisa Shields, Jennifer Anmuth, Marie X. Strauss, and Lindsay Workman provided important input and assistance. We would also like to thank Theresa Cimino and Jessica Incao at Kissinger Associates, and Beverly Sullivan and Julia Topalian at Harvard University.

Finally, we extend our thanks to the Council's president emeritus, Leslie H. Gelb. The Task Force was launched at Les's initiative, and he then played a central role in shaping its mission and membership. His successor, Richard N. Haass, immediately picked up where Les had left off, providing energy and advice as we moved from deliberation toward preparation of this report.

We believe that the Atlantic alliance remains essential to securing the core interests of Americans and Europeans alike. We hope that the efforts of this Task Force will help ensure that the Atlantic community is as vital and cohesive in this new century as it was in the last.

Henry A. Kissinger and Lawrence H. Summers, Co-Chairs
Charles A. Kupchan, Project Director

TASK FORCE REPORT

INTRODUCTION

The accomplishments of the Atlantic alliance are remarkable. History records few, if any, alliances that have yielded so many benefits for their members or for the broader international community. After centuries of recurrent conflict, war among the European great powers has become inconceivable. The Cold War has been won; the threat of nuclear war has receded. Freedom has prevailed against totalitarian ideologies. Trade, investment, and travel are more open today than ever before. Progress in raising living standards— in rich and poor countries alike—is unprecedented.

Despite these accomplishments, the transatlantic relationship is under greater strain today than at any point in at least a generation. Many Europeans assume malign intent on the part of the United States. Many Americans resent European behavior and dismiss European perceptions of today's threats. The conviction that the United States is a hyperpower to be contained has become fashionable in Europe. Reliance on coalitions of the willing to act when the United Nations and the North Atlantic Treaty Organization (NATO) will not has become the policy of the United States.

The war in Iraq brought these strains to the point of crisis. France and Germany organized resistance to the United States in the UN Security Council—alongside Russia, historically NATO's chief adversary. The Bush administration, in turn, sought to separate these states from other members of the alliance and the European Union (EU). For a time, rhetoric replaced diplomacy as the primary instrument for taking positions, making criticisms, and shaping coalitions.

These events were, to say the least, unusual. The particular outcome was influenced by domestic politics, personality, miscommunication, and unfortunate circumstance. What happened, however, was more than an intersection of unexpected developments, disputes over policy, and bad luck. The roots of the Iraq conflict extend at least as far back as 11/9, the day in 1989 when the Berlin Wall came down; they were strengthened, in turn, by the events of 9/11, the day in 2001 when terrorists destroyed the World Trade Center, attacked the Pentagon, and killed 3,000 innocent people.

When the Soviet empire in eastern Europe collapsed, the greatest reason for NATO solidarity disappeared. The subsequent unification of Germany, together with that country's peaceful integration into the alliance and the EU, deprived NATO of its clearest mission: containing and, if necessary, deterring any further expansion of Soviet influence on the continent. The alliance, in this sense, became a victim of its own success.

Threats to survival tend to concentrate minds. Without such threats, other needs loom larger in shaping the decisions of governments. The political temptation to gain advantage by criticizing or even patronizing allies increases and the urgency of maintaining a common front diminishes. Thus the end of the Cold War set Europe and the United States on separate paths when it came to defense spending, social priorities, the efficacy of military force, and even the optimal configuration of the post–Cold War world.[1]

If 11/9 increased the scope for disagreements between the United States and Europe, 9/11 created the grounds for disagreements that are truly dangerous for the transatlantic relationship. The attacks of that day produced the most sweeping reorientation of U.S. grand strategy in over half a century. Washington's goal now would be not only to contain and deter hostile states, but also to attack terrorists and regimes that harbor terrorists *before* they

---

[1]See Robert Kagan, *Of Paradise and Power: America and Europe in the New World Order* (New York: Knopf, 2003).

could act. European strategies, in contrast, underwent no comparable revision. Although NATO proclaimed solidarity with the United States in the immediate aftermath of 9/11—even to the point of invoking the previously unused Article Five of its charter, which treats an attack on one member as an attack on all—tensions within the alliance quickly escalated. The Bush administration, seeking to avoid limitations on its freedom of action, spurned offers of help in retaliating against al-Qaeda and its Taliban hosts in Afghanistan. Many NATO allies, in turn, complained of American unilateralism, while questioning the administration's insistence that the security of all nations was now at risk.

These shifts in the relationship between the United States and Europe—the consequences of 11/9 and 9/11—make it clear that the transatlantic relationship urgently needs reassessment. With the Cold War won, European integration well advanced, and new threats emerging in unconventional forms from unexpected sources, it is not surprising that differences have emerged within the transatlantic community. What is surprising is the extent to which the terrorist attacks on the United States, and the reactions of Europeans to America's response to those attacks, have transformed these differences into active confrontation. Clashes over substance and style have isolated and weakened the political constituencies that have traditionally kept Atlantic relations on course. Voices of moderation and restraint continue to confront heated dialogue, encouraging the political forces on both sides of the Atlantic that are skeptical of, if not averse to, efforts to sustain a strong transatlantic link. So too, has generational change taken a toll on the traditional pro-Atlantic constituencies.

This sequence of events therefore raises critical questions: Is the transatlantic relationship evolving into something akin to the balance-of-power system that existed prior to World War II? If so, should such a development be viewed with equanimity or alarm? Can NATO continue to exist in its present form and with its traditional focus? Can an expanding European Union cooperate with the new diplomacy of the United States? If not, what are the alternatives?

[3]

THE COMMON TRANSATLANTIC INTEREST

Alliances are means that serve ends. They are not ends in themselves. They exist to advance their members' interests, and they will survive only if those interests remain compatible. The fear that the Soviet Union might dominate post–World War II Europe produced a compatibility of interests that persisted throughout the Cold War. What comparable compatibilities exist today, within the post-11/9, post-9/11 transatlantic community?

The first and most important compatible interest, we believe, is *to maintain and support our shared traditions and the community that has formed around them.* The age of exploration saw European ideas and values transplanted to North America; the age of revolution saw constitutional democracy spread from the United States to Europe. Twice during the twentieth century, without any pre-existing alliance, Europeans and Americans elected to fight alongside one another to preserve their democratic values against authoritarian challenges. A third such challenge, that posed by the Soviet Union, required no global war, but it did produce the alliance that survives to this day. The fundamental purpose of that alliance, hence, reflects interests that preceded the Cold War, and that remain no less vital now that the Cold War is over. Europe and the United States must ensure that they remain embedded in a zone of democratic peace and that the nations of the Atlantic community are never again divided by balance-of-power competition.

A second compatible interest follows from the first: *to remove or at least neutralize whatever might place shared security and prosperity at risk.* At NATO's founding, the Soviet Union presented the clearest and most present danger to the Atlantic community. Today, the most pressing threats come from beyond Europe; the Atlantic alliance must adapt accordingly. Nonetheless, the task of consolidating peace on the European continent is not yet finished. NATO's founders were fully aware of two potential dangers that had produced great wars in the past and might yet do so in the future. One of these was aggressive nationalism, an old problem in Europe that had culminated disastrously in the rise of Nazi Germany. The other was economic protectionism: the erection of barriers to international trade, investment, and the stabilization of currencies, which had deepened the Depression of the 1930s, thereby weakening the democracies just as they needed strength. The post–World War II transatlantic relationship, crafted jointly by Europeans and Americans, sought to remove these dangers by promoting the political and economic integration of Europe. That priority too survived the end of the Cold War and today remains—because of the dangers it is meant to avoid—as compelling a common interest as it was half a century ago.

A third compatible interest grows out of the first two: *to help other parts of the world, including the Arab and Islamic world, share in the benefits of democratic institutions and market economies.* Democracy and markets have brought peace and prosperity to the Atlantic community—and hold out promise to do the same elsewhere. Europe and the United States can both set important standards and provide concrete assistance as different peoples follow their own pathways to democratic institutions and free markets.

These, we think, are the fundamentals. Neither 11/9 nor 9/11 has altered them. The Task Force's first recommendation, therefore, is a simple one: *that Europeans and Americans acknowledge what unites them and reaffirm their commitment to a common purpose.*

PRIORITIES FOR THE FUTURE

What, then, are the policy objectives the transatlantic community should set for itself if it is to ensure a future in which Europeans, Americans, and much of the rest of the world can flourish? The Task Force suggests the following priorities:

First, and most important, a world of safety, free of fear of attack from states or from organizations or individuals acting independently of states. It follows that NATO should retain its historic mission of containing and, if necessary, deterring hostile states, but it should also adapt to new kinds of threats that challenge the international state system itself. This means being prepared to contain, deter, and if necessary intervene against sources of clear and present danger. Such a mission will require the capacity to respond across a spectrum of military options; it will demand the close coordination of intelligence and police work; it will involve readiness to act "out of area" (that is, beyond NATO's existing borders); it will necessitate the flexibility to deal with dangers the nature of which no one can now foresee. The founders of the alliance knew that without security little else would be possible. That remains true today, and it will remain true well into the future.

Second, the rule of law. Americans and Europeans should seek to extend as widely as possible the institutions of civil society that originated in the United States at the end of the eighteenth century, that spread through most of Europe during the last half of the twentieth century, and that provide the indispensable underpinnings of international order in the twenty-first century. A special effort should be made to include the Arab and wider Islamic world in this undertaking. The objective here is not world government, but rather the coexistence of unity with diversity, of power with principle, of leadership with consultation, that only democratic federalism is capable of providing.

Third, the quality of life. Democratic federalism can hardly be expected to flourish when people lack the capacity to feed, clothe, house, and otherwise sustain themselves. Another heritage Europeans and Americans share is that of social responsibility: the obligation of government to provide the conditions—in terms of environment, health, education, and employment, as well as freedom of expression and equality of opportunity—upon which civil society depends. *Americans and Europeans cannot enjoy these privileges in an interconnected world without encouraging their diffusion elsewhere.* The architects of the Marshall Plan knew that without recovery there could be neither security nor law within Europe. The beneficiaries of the Marshall Plan—who include both

Europeans and Americans—have every reason to understand that this principle applies today throughout the world.

POINTS OF DIVERGENCE

If this is where the transatlantic relationship should seek to go over the next decade, then what obstacles lie in the way? There is a consensus within the transatlantic community on the numerous challenges facing common interests. These include terrorism, authoritarianism, economic incompetence, environmental degradation, and the kind of misrule that exacerbates poverty, encourages discrimination, tolerates illiteracy, allows epidemics, and proliferates weapons of mass destruction. Although there is agreement on the necessity of addressing these problems, there are differences—some easily overcome, some more serious—on how to go about doing so.

Differences over Styles of Leadership. Despite their commonalities, the two sides of the Atlantic community evolved distinctive cultures—ways of doing things—from the very beginning. These differences were sufficiently striking, by the 1830s, for Alexis de Tocqueville to examine them in *Democracy in America.* That such cultural differences should affect styles of leadership within NATO should not alarm us, however, for they have always been present in one form or another. The alliance survived such unlikely contemporaries as Lyndon B. Johnson and Charles de Gaulle; it must now overcome personality differences compounded by philosophical disputes.

Differences over Domestic Politics. Style both reflects and shapes politics, so it is natural that Europeans and Americans disagree on many domestic issues: gun control, the death penalty, genetically modified foods, tariffs, agricultural and corporate subsidies, the role of religion in politics, or the appropriate size and cost of a social welfare system. Such disputes are easily sensationalized, and positions on each side are easily caricatured. It is worth remembering, though, that the members of the transatlantic alliance are all *democracies*. It should hardly come as a surprise, then, that they differ on how best to organize or run their respective societies. That having been said, the duty of statesmen is to provide a framework in which these differences are understood rather than used, as has been the case too frequently in recent years, to demonstrate long-term incompatibility.

Differences on International Issues. Domestic differences are bound, in turn, to affect foreign policy. The United States and its European allies have disagreed sharply in recent years on such issues as the Kyoto Protocol, the International Criminal Court (ICC), the Comprehensive Test Ban Treaty (CTBT), and the Anti-Ballistic Missile (ABM) Treaty. Some perspective is warranted, however. These differences are no more serious than those that existed in the past over the Suez crisis in the 1950s, the Vietnam War in the 1960s, the Yom Kippur War and the energy crises of the 1970s, or the debate over missile deployment in the 1980s. As the handling of these past disputes made clear, they are manageable as long as they are addressed within the framework of genuinely shared strategic objectives; it is in the absence of such a framework that such disagreements have the potential to become debilitating.

Throughout the Cold War the Soviet Union served—admittedly inadvertently—as the "glue" that held NATO together. Without it, there might never have been a transatlantic alliance, to say nothing of a Truman Doctrine or a Marshall Plan. By the time the Cold War ended, cooperation was sufficiently institutionalized that there was little need for an outside threat to provide internal cohesion: NATO was intact, healthy, and expanding to the East. Its members agreed on military interventions to drive Iraq out of Kuwait in 1991, to restore order—however belatedly—in Bosnia in 1995, and to rescue the Kosovars in 1999. After 9/11, they cooperated to share intelligence, intensify anti-terrorist policing, and begin reconstruction in Afghanistan after the Americans and their local allies had ousted the Taliban. Some cooperation continues today with respect to Iran, North Korea, and the Israeli-

Palestinian conflict. This cooperation over the past decade and a half was possible because there were no fundamental disagreements among the allies on what needed to be done; differences did exist over how and when to do it. That fact made them surmountable, despite the absence of the "glue" a formidable external enemy might have provided.

On Iraq, however, there were disagreements from the start over *what was to be done*, as there had been decades earlier in the Cold War crises that strained the alliance. And this time there was no single adversary or guiding concept to encourage the resolution of differences; there was not even a consensus on what had caused the Iraqi crisis. Was it Saddam Hussein and his alleged weapons of mass destruction? Was it Osama bin Laden and al-Qaeda, perhaps in league with Saddam Hussein? Was it the Americans themselves, determined to strike out at any available target after the injuries they had suffered on 9/11? Was it the Europeans, who had remained complacent in the face of new danger? Was it the United Nations, which had oscillated between action and paralysis in dealing with the situation?

What made Iraq a distinctive and disturbing chapter in the history of the transatlantic alliance? *It was the first major crisis within the alliance to take place in the absence of an agreed-upon danger.*

LESSONS TO BE LEARNED

The Task Force believes that Europeans and Americans must now work together to ensure that the Iraq crisis becomes an anomaly in their relationship, not a precedent for things to come. The events of one year should not be allowed to disrupt a community sustained by compatible interests and common purposes over so many years. And yet, we cannot simply assume this outcome. With the end of the Cold War and the onset of the war against terrorism, the transatlantic community confronts uncharted geopolitical terrain. There is all the more reason, then, to examine its differences over Iraq carefully, to take their implications seriously, and to seek means to avoid their recurrence. Above all, the Atlantic nations should draw from the lessons of their common past.

Lesson One: No alliance can function successfully in the absence of a common strategy, or in the presence of competing strategies. For all the disagreements that took place within the NATO alliance during the Cold War, there were remarkably few over grand strategy. While the Americans usually took the lead in formulating the West's grand strategy, they rarely used their power to *impose* their views. Instead Washington officials worked hard to *persuade* allies that American positions made sense. There were a surprising number of instances in which the United States modified its own positions when those efforts at persuasion failed.[2]

The Bush administration can hardly be faulted for having been unclear about its post-9/11 grand strategy, or its intentions with respect to Iraq.[3] In contrast to its predecessors, however, it failed to win the support of key NATO members. Historians will be debating the reasons why for years to come. Was it the claim, if multilateral support was not forthcoming, to a right to unilateral action? Or was it that NATO allies and the UN Security Council failed to meet their responsibilities?

The Task Force is content to leave these questions to historians. Its chief concern, rather, is this: that an alliance has meaning only when its members adjust their policies to take into account their partners' interests—when they do things for one another that they would not do if the alliance did not exist. If the transatlantic relationship is to continue to mean what it has meant in the past, both sides must learn from their failure over Iraq. The Americans will need to reaffirm the insight that shaped their approach to allies throughout the Cold War: that the power to act is not

---

[2]For the historical record, see John Lewis Gaddis, *We Now Know: Rethinking Cold War History* (New York: Oxford University Press, 1997), pp. 200–203.

[3]See especially President George W. Bush's speech to the UN General Assembly, September 12, 2002, and *The National Security Strategy of the United States of America*, released by the White House on September 17, 2002.

necessarily the power to persuade; that even in an alliance in which military capabilities are disproportionately distributed, the costs of unilateralism can exceed those involved in seeking consent. The Europeans, in turn, will need to acknowledge that the post-9/11 world is by no means safe for transatlantic societies, that the dangers that make it unsafe do not come from Washington, and that neither nostalgia for the past nor insularity in the present will suffice in coping with those threats. The objective is not so much a formal consensus—the quest for which can be debilitating and paralyzing—but a common sense of direction.

Lesson Two: A common strategy need not require equivalent capabilities. One of the reasons NATO succeeded during the Cold War was that it acknowledged complementarity. It was clear from the outset that Europe would never match the Americans' military capabilities, or their ability to deploy their forces on a global scale. Instead the Europeans focused on economic reconstruction, integration, and consolidating the benefits these provided. By the end of the Cold War, they had assumed a heavier burden than the United States in providing aid to developing countries, assuming international policing and peacekeeping responsibilities, and supporting international organizations. These asymmetries are now embedded on both sides of the Atlantic, and any revitalization of the alliance will have to respect them.

The way to do this, the Task Force believes, is to regard complementarity as an asset, not a liability. If the United States is the indispensable nation in terms of its military power, then surely the Europeans are indispensable allies in most of the other categories of power upon which statecraft depends. Whether the issues are countering terrorism, liberalizing trade, preventing international crime, containing weapons of mass destruction, rebuilding post-conflict states, combating poverty, fighting disease, or spreading democracy and human rights, European and American priorities and capabilities complement one another far more often than they compete with one another.

This pattern broke down over Iraq—with unfortunate consequences. The Task Force believes strongly that there is no alternative to complementarity, and that if the transatlantic alliance is to recover and prosper, its members will need to rediscover this principle and revive its practice. That means, for the Europeans, abandoning the pretension that their power as currently constituted can bring about multipolarity or that confrontation is the best way to influence the United States. For America, it means recalling that military strength alone did not win the Cold War. Rather, victory came about because the multidimensional power of the United States and its allies ultimately prevailed over the Soviet Union's single dimension of strength—its military power.

While respecting complementarity is crucial to the Atlantic alliance, an absolute division of labor is not viable. If the Europeans focus their attention on peacekeeping and nation-building while the United States assumes all the responsibility for more demanding military tasks, this division of labor will prove politically divisive: Americans will sooner or later resent the greater risks and burdens they have assumed, while Europeans will object to their ancillary role. In addition, the inability to act in unison would over time mean that Europeans and Americans would less frequently share common tasks and experiences—inevitably reinforcing divergent viewpoints.

Lesson Three: The maintenance of a healthy Atlantic alliance requires domestic political leadership. One of the developments that most concerns the Task Force has been the sharp upturn in anti-American sentiment in many European countries[4]—no doubt one of

---

[4]For the results of public opinion surveys, see the Pew Research Center for the People and the Press, "America's Image Further Erodes, Europeans Want Weaker Ties," March 18, 2003, available at http://people-press.org/reports/display.php3?ReportID=175; "Americans and Europeans Differ Widely on Foreign Policy Issues," April 17, 2002, available at http://people-press.org/reports/display.php3?ReportID=153; "Bush Unpopular in Europe, Seen as Unilateralist," August 15, 2001, available at http://people-press.org/reports/display.php3?ReportID=5; German Marshall Fund of the United States and the Compagnia di San Paolo, "Transatlantic Trends 2003," September 4, 2003, available at www.transatlantictrends.org; and German Marshall Fund of the United States and the Chicago Council on Foreign Relations, "Worldviews 2002," September 4, 2002, available at www.worldviews.org. See also Thomas Crampton, "Europeans' doubt over U.S. policy rises," *International Herald Tribune,* September 4, 2003.

the reasons politicians there chose to embrace it. Although not quite as apparent, anti-European views—particularly directed against France and Germany—have grown within the United States as well.

When similar situations arose during the Cold War, leaders on both sides of the Atlantic made visible gestures to repair rifts, strengthen institutions, and reaffirm their commitment to a lasting partnership. Such leadership is needed now to lower the rhetorical temperature by reminding Europeans and Americans of how much there is to lose from continued transatlantic tension, and how much there is to gain from effective collaboration.

If the United States is to succeed in achieving its primary objectives in the world, whether those objectives be the successful confrontation of terror, ensuring the preservation of peace and prosperity, or the spreading of democracy, Americans must recognize that they cannot succeed alone. Without the leverage provided by protection from the communist threat, the United States must find other means of influence over nations. Legitimacy matters over time and it depends on international support. And without European support, it is not possible to imagine the United States assembling meaningful coalitions of other nations.

Likewise the Atlantic alliance serves fundamental European interests. The world remains a dangerous place and the American capacity to project force is not likely to be matched in the next several decades. If the United States and Europe do not find an effective modus vivendi there will inevitably be increasing tensions within Europe as different nations take different views on actions taken by the United States. Nor is the most visionary of European projects—the gradual extension of international law and institutions to the global community on the model of what has happened in Europe over the past half-century—a viable concept without the cooperation of the United States.

European elites today rarely recount the role the United States played in saving European democracy, reviving European prosperity, encouraging European integration, and continuing to provide European security. American elites rarely acknowledge that the European Union has stabilized democracy, facilitating the enlargement of NATO and free markets, and promoted tolerance in central and eastern Europe; or that Europe now provides the bulk of troops and assistance in the Balkans and in Afghanistan; or that the EU and its member states give much more in direct development aid than does the United States. Public recognition of these accomplishments by leaders on both sides of the Atlantic—in statements, in speeches, possibly in a "New Atlantic Charter"— would go far toward dampening disturbing swings in public opinion. They also happen to be achievements of which Europeans and Americans have every right to be proud.

Lesson Four: The time has come to clarify the purposes and benefits of European integration. For the past half-century, the United States has supported the principle of European unification, viewing that process as the best method for diminishing the risk of devastating wars, enhancing the prospects of democratization, expanding international trade and investment, ensuring prosperity, and building a more effective transatlantic alliance. Alongside their support for European unity, however, American leaders have long harbored a certain ambivalence.

While they have hoped to see Europe stand on its own without American support, they have also feared that it might do just that, thereby weakening the influence the United States has enjoyed in Europe and challenging American interests elsewhere. As Europe's strategic dependence on the United States has lessened with the end of the Cold War, these American concerns have become more pronounced. The Iraq crisis further magnified them, especially after France and Germany tried to organize a global coalition to resist the Bush administration's decision to invade that country.

Meanwhile, Europe itself divided over Iraq, with France and Germany finding themselves at odds with several current and prospective EU members—most conspicuously Great Britain, Italy,

Spain, and Poland—who supported the position of the United States. Not surprisingly, these trends produced a greater emphasis in Washington on bilateral rather than multilateral relations both in the run-up to the war and in the management of its aftermath. American ambivalence toward European integration also intensified.

The pace and scope of European integration are matters for Europeans to decide. But the American response to this process will be affected by how the EU's leaders and electorates perceive the union's role. Casting the EU as a counterweight to the United States, even if only for rhetorical purposes, will surely fuel transatlantic tension and encourage Washington to look elsewhere for international partners. If, however, the EU frames its policies in complementary terms, as it has done in the past, Washington should continue to regard Europe's deepening and widening as in America's interest. A deeper Europe could ensure the irreversibility of union and could lead to a more militarily capable EU—one that could in time become a more effective partner of the United States. A wider Europe could ensure that peace, democracy, and prosperity continue to spread eastward, thereby converging with what could be similar trends in Russia.

The debate over multipolarity transcends the tactical issue of U.S.-European relations. It goes to the heart of the emerging international order. A unifying Europe will be a growing force in international relations; it is beyond America's capacity and against its interest to attempt to thwart it. In that sense, Europe's evolution contributes to multipolarity. But if Europe defines its identity in terms of countering U.S. power, the world is likely to return to a balance-of-power system reminiscent of the era prior to World War I—with the same disastrous consequences. National interest is a crucial component of foreign policy. Should every actor in the international system seek to maximize only its own interest, however, constant tension is a more likely outcome than world order. The strength of the alliance depends on fostering attitudes that see the common interest as compatible with the national interest.

Despite the EU's aspirations, European weakness is likely to present more of a problem for the transatlantic partnership than European strength. The EU still falls short of unity on matters of foreign policy, and its military capability, despite recent reforms, remains quite limited. The impending entry of ten new members is bound to absorb its attention and resources over the next several years; that task may delay progress toward forging a common European security policy and acquiring the assets needed to back it up.

Both sides of the Atlantic, therefore, have important roles to play in shaping the future of the EU. American leaders must resolve their long-standing ambivalence about the emerging European entity. Europe's leaders must resist the temptation to define its identity in opposition to the United States. Those who believe in Atlantic partnership need to be heard calling for a Europe that remains a steady partner of the United States, even as it strengthens itself and broadens its international role.

Lesson Five: Transatlantic economic cooperation reinforces political cooperation. The U.S.-European relationship has been grounded in economic cooperation since the earliest days of the Cold War: the Marshall Plan, after all, preceded NATO. Today the American and European economies are the world's largest, and they are likely to remain so for the foreseeable future. Transatlantic commerce approaches $2.5 trillion per year and employs directly or indirectly some twelve million workers in Europe and the United States.[5] Although there have been frequent disputes over tariffs and subsidies through the years, the Task Force notes that the Iraqi crisis had little discernible effect on patterns of European-American trade and investment.

That fact suggests that a greater public emphasis on the economic benefits of the relationship might help leaders on both sides of the Atlantic resolve, or at least minimize, their political differ-

---

[5] Joseph Quinlan, "Drifting Apart or Growing Together? The Primacy of the Transatlantic Economy," Center for Transatlantic Relations, Washington, D.C., 2003, p. 3.

ences. The U.S. and European economies depend heavily on one another; together they have a major impact on the international economy as a whole. The prospects for sustained expansion will be much greater if the movement toward integrating global trade and investment continues to move forward. This can hardly happen without a common U.S.-European approach. Nor, in the absence of such cooperation, is there likely to be a long-term strategy for fostering economic progress and the political liberalization it can bring within the developing world. Without such a strategy, Americans and Europeans are likely to find themselves struggling with the consequences of illiberal regimes and failed states instead of attacking their root causes.

It remains as true today as when the postwar transatlantic community first emerged, therefore, that politics and economics are intertwined. This too is a complementarity upon which the future of the U.S.-European relationship will surely depend.

THE BROADER AGENDA

The transatlantic relationship cannot be isolated from the larger international system of which it is a part. The Task Force believes that any efforts to revitalize the alliance must also take into account the precedents these may set—and the responsibilities these may imply—for the global community as a whole. The United States and its allies largely defined the post–World War II international order. The end of the Cold War and the events of September 11 have challenged that system's guiding norms, but they have not diminished the role Americans and Europeans will have to play in reasserting them. The path toward a renewal of transatlantic accord, therefore, could well lie beyond the transatlantic arena.

This challenge is often defined as a need to improve the process of consultation. But this is only the formal aspect of the problem. Consultation should become more regular and more focused on longer-term issues. But, above all, it needs to be understood that the test will be the emergence of a set of common purposes.

The Task Force suggests the following priorities for the United States, the NATO alliance, and Europe, as a basis for their relationship with the rest of the world.

Establish New Guidelines for the Use of Military Force. Over the past half-century, a hallmark of transatlantic partnership has been agreement on basic principles governing the employment of military capabilities. Today, new challenges require a reassessment of those principles. Terrorism, the proliferation of weapons of mass destruction, and the emergence of cooperation between irresponsible states and nonstate actors have raised the question of whether a strategy aimed at forestalling potentially dangerous adversaries *before* they can strike should supplement familiar Cold War "rules of engagement"—the containment and deterrence of potentially hostile states. The issue is not an easy one to resolve. On the one hand, it is hard to imagine a stable world in which all nations claim the right to launch a preventive war based on their own threat assessments. On the other hand, it is difficult to maintain that any nation can completely cede decisions fundamental to its own safety to an international community that may lack the resources and resolve for decisive action.

The Atlantic alliance can help to solve this problem by establishing "rules of the road" regarding preventive uses of military force. These could begin with a consensus on what *not* to do: for example, Europeans could agree not to reject preventive action in principle, while Americans would agree that prevention (or "preemption," in the usage of the Bush administration) would be reserved for special cases and not be the centerpiece of U.S. strategy. Both parties could then acknowledge the progress that has already been made in specifying the conditions in which intervention is justified: to combat terrorism (as in Afghanistan), to back multilaterally sanctioned inspections (as in Iraq), or to achieve humanitarian goals (as in Bosnia, Kosovo, and East Timor). Recent EU planning documents have called for robust action to forestall threats from terrorism and weapons of mass destruction, as has UN Secretary-

General Kofi Annan.[6] These trends suggest that the United States, NATO, the EU, and the UN might find more common ground on this issue than one might expect from the rhetoric. Determining whether these converging views could produce a formal agreement on basic principles would be well worth the effort.

Develop a Common Policy toward Irresponsible States. Preventive strikes should always be a last resort. The transatlantic alliance should also agree on how to forestall situations that might require it. That means developing compatible policies toward states that possess or seek to possess weapons of mass destruction, that harbor terrorists or support terrorism, and that seek through these means to challenge the international order that Europeans and Americans have created and must sustain.

Since the Cold War ended the two communities have drifted apart in their approaches to irresponsible states. American leaders have generally favored containment and, if necessary, confrontation while their European counterparts have preferred negotiation and, if possible, accommodation. As with guidelines for the use of military force, both sides need to adjust their policies to take into account each other's views.

Europeans should acknowledge the need for credible threats, not just inducements, in dealing with irresponsible states: coercive diplomacy is at times necessary to achieve results. Americans need to be prepared to include inducements in their strategy: threats do not in all instances produce acquiescence. The fact that there is no consensus on what caused Libya—once on everyone's list of irresponsible states—to abandon its efforts to acquire weapons of mass destruction suggests the wisdom of including both sticks and carrots in any transatlantic solution to this problem. So too does the less dramatic but no less significant progress that has been made in seeking to slow or halt nuclear programs in Iran.

---

[6]See, for example, "Basic Principles for an EU Strategy against Weapons of Mass Destruction," Council of Ministers, June 2003, 10352/03, and Javier Solana, "A Secure Europe in a Better World," Council of Ministers, June 2003, S0138/03; Kofi Annan speech to the UN General Assembly, September 23, 2003.

The Atlantic partners need to ensure that their search for common ground does not become a pretext for procrastination, thereby providing irresponsible states more time to develop their weapons capabilities. Ongoing initiatives should therefore be stepped up, including deepening cooperation on securing nuclear materials in the former Soviet Union; strengthening links between U.S. and European intelligence services; expanding the recently launched naval search-and-seizure program more formally known as the Proliferation Security Initiative; closing loopholes in the non-proliferation regime that allow countries to legally accumulate stockpiles of nuclear fuel; and tightening enforcement mechanisms to respond to violations of existing counterproliferation regimes.

Agree on the Role of Multilateral Institutions. Disagreement over the efficacy and responsibility of international institutions has been a major source of transatlantic discord since at least the mid-1990s. Disputes over the CTBT, the Kyoto Protocol, the ICC, and the ABM Treaty were straining European-American relations well before 9/11 and the crisis over Iraq. In the aftermath of those events, there is now a growing sentiment in Europe—and among critics of the Bush administration within the United States—that Americans are becoming uncompromising unilateralists, while Europeans are seen by their American detractors as uncritical and naïve multilateralists whose real aim is to constrain American power.

These perceptions miss the nature of the problem. Disagreements on policy, not differences over the utility of international institutions, have caused most of these clashes. Had Americans and Europeans reached a consensus on the issues involved, disputes over procedure would have seemed much less serious, and the UN debate over Iraq would likely have found an agreed outcome. To be sure, Europe's enthusiasm for multilateralism does reflect its success in subordinating national sovereignty to international institutions: given the continent's previous history, this is an impressive accomplishment. But Europe's experience is not an automatic precedent for every part of the world. America's ambivalence toward multilateralism no doubt stems from its primacy within the international system, as well as a tradition that has always valued freedom from external constraint. But it is not a congenital attitude. The League of Nations, the United Nations, the International Monetary Fund and the World Bank, NATO, and the EU might never have been established had it not been for American support. As the experiences of World War II and the Cold War made clear, when the United States and its European allies agree on policy objectives, the institutional frameworks for implementing them usually follow.

There are compelling reasons now, on both sides of the Atlantic, to revive this tradition of function determining form. Europe will find international institutions much less effective if the world's only superpower has stepped away from them. The United States loses support abroad when it is seen to be acting unilaterally, making it harder for Washington to enlist allies in pursuing its objectives and in marshaling domestic support.[7] The transatlantic alliance will surely need greater flexibility in managing international institutions than it did during the Cold War. With NATO soon to have twenty-six members, decision-making will need to incorporate—as the EU already does—procedures for abstention, opting out of specific missions, and assembling "coalitions of the willing." Constructive ambiguity can help, as it already has in arranging the EU's use of NATO assets and Russia's participation in NATO deliberations. Nor is such ambiguity alien to the history of NATO: the alliance could hardly have survived without it.

The United States and its European allies do need to reestablish the habit of frequent, frank, and timely consultation. Diplomatic contacts at top levels must be restored.[8] Institutionalized contact groups can promote routine consultation and facilitate the accom-

---

[7]See, for example, question 7\g, p. 21, German Marshall Fund of the United States and the Compagnia di San Paolo, "Transatlantic Trends 2003," September 4, 2003, available at www.transatlantictrends.org.

[8]For more on this problem, see Philip Gordon and Jeremy Shapiro, *Allies at War: America, Europe, and the Crisis over Iraq* (New York: McGraw-Hill, 2004).

modation of respective policy positions. The potential of ad hoc groups, such as the Quartet in the Middle East, should be fully exploited. To broaden the legitimacy of joint initiatives, whether they emerge through formal procedures or through informal diplomacy, the United States and European countries should explore widening the circle of consultation by developing a "caucus of democracies." This caucus, drawing on the existing Community of Democracies launched in Warsaw in 2000, could address questions of UN reform as well as a broader range of diplomatic issues.

Build a Common Approach to the Greater Middle East. The greater Middle East—the region stretching from North Africa to Southwest Asia—is the part of the world with the greatest potential to affect the security and prosperity of Europeans and Americans alike. The region contains the globe's greatest concentration of oil and natural gas. It poses potent threats from international terrorism and the proliferation of weapons of mass destruction. The region faces a rapidly rising youth population—for example, roughly 50 percent of Saudi Arabia's population is under the age of twenty— but economies ill suited to providing gainful employment. Europe's proximity to the greater Middle East and its growing Muslim population make these issues all the more urgent.

The transatlantic community must tackle four central issues, the first of which is Iraq. Leaders on both sides of the Atlantic have already agreed that the provision of security, the establishment of a stable and legitimate government, and the expeditious reconstruction of that country are vital objectives. Failure to achieve these objectives would lead to severe consequences for all members of the alliance. To realize these goals, Europeans and Americans must set aside narrow political and economic ambitions in the region and jointly shoulder responsibility for stabilizing the country.

NATO, already demonstrating its value in Afghanistan, is a natural successor to the current international military presence in Iraq. If a substantial increase in financial and military support from Europe is to be forthcoming, the United States must be prepared for greater European participation in the political management of Iraq. Moving forward, an active and constructive transatlantic dialogue on these issues must be sustained.

Iran is a second issue. Iran is experiencing considerable internal debate over the direction of its domestic politics and foreign policy. Americans and Europeans should coordinate their policies—if possible, with Russia as well—to ensure that Iranians fully understand how the international community will react to their decisions regarding proliferation, support for terrorism, and democracy. The importance of encouraging political reform in Iran and neutralizing potential threats should give Europe and the United States a strong incentive to act in unison.

A third issue is the Israeli-Palestinian conflict. The widespread perception in Europe that the United States one-sidedly favors Israel weakens support for American foreign policy in Europe. Meanwhile, many American policymakers see European policy toward the dispute as reflexively pro-Palestinian. Both sides need to make an effort to achieve a common position. The United States needs to define more precisely its concept of a Palestinian state; Europe must take more seriously Israel's concern for security.

A fourth area for transatlantic cooperation in the greater Middle East concerns the area's long-term economic and political development. Many countries in the region have lagged behind the rest of the world in moving toward democratic societies and market economies. Educational systems are in many instances not providing the skills needed for competing successfully in the modern world; women often are denied basic rights and opportunities. The rigid and brittle societies that result breed widespread frustration and disaffection—social characteristics conducive to radicalism and terrorism. Such societies are also prone to state failure, civil war, or both.

Tackling these challenges requires a concerted effort by Europe and the United States, one comparable to the effort waged during the Cold War to assist and win over much of the developing world. Such an undertaking requires considerable resources over a sustained period. It also requires astute public diplomacy. The goal should be not to impose change on traditional societies, but rather to work with local political, economic, and civic leaders in supporting a gradual process of reform.

FORGING A FUTURE TRANSATLANTIC SECURITY RELATIONSHIP

The new strategic landscape necessitates a transatlantic security partnership that builds upon—but does not uncritically imitate—the one that won the Cold War. The core principles of that alliance were the indivisibility of security and a shared commitment to collective defense. In practice, this meant a massive deployment of U.S. military forces in Europe, together with support for European economic and political integration. The objective was to contain any further expansion of Soviet influence in Europe, while building a Europe that could in time become a great power in its own right.

Today NATO's principles remain valid, but not all of its historic practices do. There is no further need for a large American military presence in the middle of Europe; redeployments elsewhere are already taking place. The threats confronting the alliance are more diverse than they were during the Cold War; hence American and European security interests will no longer correspond as precisely as they once did.

To this end, the Task Force looks forward to a NATO alliance that is at once more flexible in its procedures and more ambitious in its missions than it has been in the past. Among its tasks should be:

Continuing to Serve as the Primary Forum for Transatlantic Cooperation on International Security. Even as the United States draws down the number of its troops deployed on the continent, it should maintain a sufficient presence to ensure both the interoperability and the sense of collective purpose that arises from an integrated military structure. At the same time, it must be more receptive to EU efforts to assume a more prominent role in the management of European security. The overall direction of policy should be clear: that the United States continues to welcome what it has sought since the earliest days of the Cold War— a Europe in which Europeans bear the primary responsibility for their own security.

Britain, France, and Germany are taking the lead on this front, and next steps include the establishment of an EU planning headquarters that is separate from NATO. The United States has stated its opposition to changes that threaten the integrity of NATO command, and there are serious questions about how an EU headquarters separate from NATO might work. Specifically, will the EU members of NATO vote as a bloc and prior to NATO consultation? And, if so, do we reach a point where consultation turns into institutional confrontation? How will NATO and the EU define their respective missions and will the EU proceed with military operations only after NATO has decided not to do so? Until the questions are answered, irrevocable decisions should be avoided.

Facilitating the Consolidation of Peace, Democracy, and Prosperity in Eastern and Southeastern Europe. The 1990s made it painfully clear that a stable peace has yet to take root in some parts of Europe, and NATO's tasks in the Balkans are far from over. Even as the EU gradually assumes peacekeeping responsibilities in Bosnia, Kosovo, and Macedonia, a NATO presence will be required there to prevent backsliding and to help resolve residual political and territorial disputes. The alliance must also encourage reform and integration in Turkey, Ukraine, and Russia. Turkey's membership in NATO has long strengthened that country's westward orientation; openness to increasing other links between Turkey and Europe would similarly prove constructive. The prospect of joining NATO has promoted reform in Ukraine, as it has elsewhere in eastern Europe. The NATO-Russia Council has given Moscow a voice in the alliance and contributed to a new level of cooperation between Russia, Europe, and the United States. The momentum behind all of these initiatives must be kept up.

Adjusting to New Geopolitical Realities. NATO must recognize the extent to which the aftermaths of 11/9 and 9/11 transformed the strategic priorities of the United States. As the United States redeploys its forces outside of Europe, the alliance must find the appropriate balance between a new emphasis on out-of-area missions and its traditional focus on European security. Although NATO will continue to remain active both within and outside the geographical confines of Europe, there needs to be a common understanding that NATO must increasingly concern itself with threats emanating from outside Europe if the alliance is to prove as central to the post-11/9 (and post-9/11) world as it was throughout the Cold War.

Managing the Global Economy. As the task of reconstructing Iraq suggests, NATO's responsibilities extend well beyond the military realm. Its history has always paralleled that of the EU and will surely continue to do so. For this reason, security cooperation requires economic cooperation. It follows, then, that Europeans and Americans must work together, not just to liberalize U.S.-European trade, but also to ensure the successful completion of the current round of world trade negotiations. High-level consultations designed to produce a common approach to the Doha round are essential.

Europeans and Americans must also pursue a long-term strategy for fostering economic growth and political liberalization in the developing world. Specific elements of such a strategy should include eliminating trade barriers with developing regions, particularly in the agricultural and textile sectors, and improving coordination among the assistance programs of individual countries, nongovernmental organizations, and major international institutions in order to increase efficiency and minimize waste. Europe should create an analogue to the Millennium Challenge Account so that American and European grants of economic assistance are made conditional on the same governance reforms and directed in a manner that maximizes their impact. Similarly, both Europeans and Americans should increase and coordinate their assistance to local and global efforts to combat HIV/AIDS and other infectious diseases.

CONCLUSION

The Task Force is fully aware of the difficulties efforts to restore the full spirit of transatlantic partnership will face. In the absence of clear and present dangers to focus their minds, European and American leaders will undoubtedly be tempted to cater to groups within their respective societies who have little interest in encouraging, and may actively oppose, transatlantic cooperation. American leaders seeking to satisfy those who favor a freer hand will downplay the benefits of partnership. European leaders who wish to appeal to pacifism will distance themselves from the United States. Opportunists are likely to see the promotion of anti-American or anti-European sentiments as a way to advance their own interests. Governments on both sides of the Atlantic will surely face pressure to protect domestic economic interests from foreign competition, and history suggests that they will—all too often—succumb to these pressures. On some issues, moreover, there will be legitimate conflicts of interest, and little or no chance of achieving consensus.

The Task Force is convinced, however, that the approach outlined above will appeal to a multiparty, pragmatic majority in all countries of the Western alliance. The Task Force also believes that leaders who embrace it will be rewarded rather than penalized by their publics. Articulating a vision for the Atlantic community and sustaining a commitment to it will challenge European and American leaders alike, but it is hardly a greater challenge than Western democracies have surmounted in the past.

Farsighted vision and political courage sustained the transatlantic partnership for half a century, to the overwhelming benefit of Europeans, Americans, and the world. Today's challenges are different, but the benefits of partnership are still substantial—as are the costs if the partnership is allowed to erode. Recent acrimony demonstrates not only the difficulties that arise for America and Europe when they fail to act as partners, but also that pressing problems are best addressed together. In the end, Europe and America have far more to gain as allies than as neutrals or adversaries. We are confident that with enlightened leadership, governments and citizens on both sides of the Atlantic will grasp and act upon that reality.

ADDITIONAL VIEW

The Task Force report identifies many of the core problems facing Europe and the United States and offers useful prescriptions for dealing with them. While endorsing its main recommendations, I would also note three problems.

First, the report does not give sufficient weight to the structural forces that are pulling Europe and the United States apart. The dispute over Iraq was unusual, but it was also the most intense manifestation of a downward trend that began when the Soviet threat disappeared. The report attributes these disputes to "personality differences" and "philosophical disputes." But asymmetry of power—not philosophy—is the root cause of this dispute: if the power relationship between Europe and America were reversed, Europe would find hegemony appealing and the United States would desire a more multipolar structure. U.S. and European conceptions of the national interest differ for this reason: Europeans *will* try to constrain U.S. power, and Americans *will* resent it when they do. Adroit statecraft may be able to manage these conflicting interests, but it is going to be harder than the report suggests.

Second, the report calls for greater cooperation in addressing problems in the Middle East, including Iraq, the social ills of the Arab and Islamic world, and the Israeli-Palestinian conflict. Yet it lacks a sense of urgency about these issues, especially with respect to the latter issue. America's role in this prolonged conflict has done great damage to the U.S. image in Europe and elsewhere. Yet the report merely calls for Europe and America to "make an effort to achieve a common position." It also recommends that the United States "define more precisely its concept of a Palestinian state" and that Europe "take more seriously Israel's concern for security," but these steps are hardly sufficient to break the current impasse. By failing to spell out how the United States and Europe could cooperate to fashion a just and durable settlement, the Task Force missed an obvious opportunity.

Third, the report repeats the unsupported claim that Osama bin Laden, al-Qaeda, and Saddam Hussein might somehow have been "in league." This statement is used for rhetorical purposes (i.e., in a discussion of competing views about the origins of the Iraq crisis), but to include it without rebuttal suggests that it might have some legitimate basis. In fact, there is no credible evidence to support this claim, and it is regrettable that a Council on Foreign Relations Task Force report may unwittingly reinforce widespread public confusion on this issue.

Stephen M. Walt

TASK FORCE MEMBERS

GIULIANO AMATO is a Member of the Italian Senate, Global Law Professor at the New York University Law School, and part-time Professor at the European University Institute in Florence. He held several ministerial positions in the Italian government and was Prime Minister twice. He also headed the Italian Antitrust Authority and was Vice-President of the Convention on the Future of Europe. He currently chairs an International Commission on the Balkans under the auspices of the Bosch Stiftung, the German Marshall Fund, and the King Baudouin Foundation.

REGINALD BARTHOLOMEW is Vice Chairman of Merrill Lynch Europe. He was U.S. Ambassador to Lebanon, Spain, NATO, and Italy, and served as Undersecretary of State for International Security Affairs.

DOUGLAS K. BEREUTER is a Republican Member of Congress from Nebraska. He is the Chairman of the Europe Subcommittee of the House International Relations Committee, the Vice Chairman of the House Permanent Select Committee on Intelligence, and the President of the NATO Parliamentary Assembly.

HAROLD BROWN is a Partner at Warburg Pincus and Counselor at the Center for Strategic and International Studies. He served as Secretary of Defense during the Carter administration and is President Emeritus of the California Institute of Technology.

RICHARD R. BURT serves as Chairman of Diligence LLC. He is also a Senior Adviser to the Center for Strategic and International Studies and Chairman of the American Committee of the International Institute for Strategic Studies. Mr. Burt was the U.S. Chief Negotiator in the Strategic Arms Reduction Talks

---

Note: Task Force members participate in their individual and not institutional capacities.

[31]

(START) with the former Soviet Union. Prior to this, he was
U.S. Ambassador to the Federal Republic of Germany (1985–89).
Before Mr. Burt served in Germany, he worked at the State Department as Assistant Secretary of State for European and Canadi-
an Affairs.

THIERRY DE MONTBRIAL is the Founder and President of IFRI (the
French Institute of International Relations). He is also Professor of Economics and International Relations at the Conserva-
toire National des Arts et Métiers in Paris. Professor de Montbrial
was Director of the Policy Planning Staff in the French Min-
istry of Foreign Affairs (1973–79) and Chairman of the Paris-based
Foundation for Strategic Studies (1993–2001).

THOMAS E. DONILON is Executive Vice President and Member
of the Office of the Chairman at Fannie Mae. Previously, he was
a Partner at the international law firm of O'Melveny & Myers.
Mr. Donilon served as Assistant Secretary of State and Chief
of Staff at the State Department during the first Clinton
administration.

STUART E. EIZENSTAT is the head of international trade and
finance at Covington & Burling, a Washington-based law firm.
He was U.S. Ambassador to the European Union (1993–96);
Undersecretary of Commerce for International Trade (1996–97);
Undersecretary of State for Economic, Business, and Agricul-
tural Affairs (1997–99); Deputy Secretary of the Treasury
(1999–2001) in the Clinton administration; as well as Special Rep-
resentative of the President on Holocaust Issues. He was Chief
Domestic Policy Adviser and Executive Director of the White
House Domestic Policy Staff in the Carter administration.

MARTIN FELDSTEIN is the George F. Baker Professor of Economics at Harvard University and President and CEO of the
National Bureau of Economic Research. He is also President of
the American Economic Association for 2004. From 1982
through 1984, he was Chairman of the Council of Economic Advisers and President Ronald Reagan's chief economic adviser.

JOHN LEWIS GADDIS is Robert A. Lovett Professor of History and Political Science at Yale University, where he teaches Cold War history, grand strategy, international studies, and biography. He was the 2003 recipient of the Phi Beta Kappa award for undergraduate teaching at Yale. His most recent book is *Surprise, Security, and the American Experience.*

TIMOTHY GARTON ASH is Director of the European Studies Centre at St. Antony's College, Oxford University, and a Senior Fellow of the Hoover Institution, Stanford University. He is the author of many books and articles on contemporary European history and politics. His latest book, *Free World: America, Europe, and the Future of the West,* will be published by Random House in the fall of 2004.

G. JOHN IKENBERRY is the Peter F. Krogh Professor of Geopolitics and Global Justice at Georgetown University. In July 2004, Ikenberry will become Professor of Public and International Affairs in the Woodrow Wilson School of Public and International Affairs and the Politics Department at Princeton University. He has previously held posts on the State Department's Policy Planning Staff during the first Bush administration and at the Carnegie Endowment for International Peace. During 2002–2004, Professor Ikenberry is a Transatlantic Fellow at the German Marshall Fund. He is the author of *After Victory: Institutions, Strategic Restraint, and the Rebuilding of Order after Major Wars,* which won the 2002 Schroeder-Jervis Award presented by the American Political Science Association for the best book in international history and politics. He is also the reviewer of books on political and legal affairs for *Foreign Affairs.*

JOSEF JOFFE is Editor of *Die Zeit* in Hamburg, Germany. He is also an Associate of the Olin Institute for Strategic Studies at Harvard and a Research Fellow of the Hoover Institution at Stanford University. Previously, he was Editorial Page Editor of the *Süddeutsche Zeitung* in Munich. He has held visiting appointments at Johns Hopkins University, Harvard University, Princeton University, and Stanford University.

ROBERT KAGAN is Senior Associate at the Carnegie Endowment for International Peace. He writes a monthly column on world affairs for the *Washington Post* and is a Contributing Editor at both the *Weekly Standard* and the *New Republic*. Kagan served in the State Department from 1984 to 1988 as a member of the Policy Planning Staff, as principal speechwriter for Secretary of State George P. Shultz, and as Deputy for Policy in the Bureau of Inter-American Affairs. He is a graduate of Yale University and Harvard University's John F. Kennedy School of Government.

HENRY A. KISSINGER is Co-chair of the Task Force and Chairman of Kissinger Associates, Inc., an international consulting firm. He was Secretary of State from 1973 to 1977, serving under Presidents Richard Nixon and Gerald Ford. He also served as Assistant to the President for National Security Affairs from 1969 to 1975. He has since served on a number of U.S. government boards and commissions including the President's Foreign Intelligence Advisory Board and the Defense Policy Board.

CHARLES A. KUPCHAN is Director of the Task Force and Senior Fellow and Director of Europe Studies at the Council on Foreign Relations. He is also an Associate Professor of International Relations at Georgetown University. Dr. Kupchan was Director for European Affairs on the National Security Council (NSC) during the first Clinton administration. Before joining the NSC, he worked in the U.S. Department of State on the Policy Planning Staff.

SYLVIA MATHEWS is Chief Operating Officer and Executive Director of the Bill & Melinda Gates Foundation. Before joining the Gates Foundation, Mathews served in the Clinton administration as Deputy Director of the Office of Management and Budget. Mathews also served as Assistant to the President and Deputy Chief of Staff to the President, and as Chief of Staff to Secretary of the Treasury Robert E. Rubin.

ANDREW MORAVCSIK is Professor of Government and Director of the European Union Center at Harvard University. Dr. Moravcsik has served as a trade negotiator at the U.S. Commerce Department, as Editor-in-Chief of a Washington foreign policy journal, and on the staff of the Deputy Prime Minister of South Korea.

ANDRZEJ OLECHOWSKI is a leader of Civic Platform, a centrist Polish political party. He was Minister of Foreign Affairs (1993–95) and Minister of Finance (1992) of Poland.

FELIX G. ROHATYN served as U.S. Ambassador to France from 1997 to 2000. Prior to that, he was Managing Director of the investment banking firm Lazard Freres & Co., LLC, in New York, where he had worked for nearly fifty years. Ambassador Rohatyn also served as Chairman of the Municipal Assistance Corporation of the State of New York, where he managed negotiations that enabled New York City to solve its financial crisis in the 1970s. He has served as a Member of the Board of Governors of the New York Stock Exchange and as a Director of a number of American and French corporations. He is a Trustee of the Center for Strategic and International Studies and a member of the Council on Foreign Relations. Currently, Ambassador Rohatyn is President of Rohatyn Associates LLC in New York.

BRENT SCOWCROFT served as Assistant to the President for National Security Affairs for Presidents George H.W. Bush and Gerald Ford. A retired U.S. Air Force Lieutenant General, General Scowcroft served in numerous national security posts in the Pentagon and the White House prior to his appointments as Assistant to the President for National Security Affairs. He also held a number of teaching positions at West Point and the Air Force Academy, specializing in political science. General Scowcroft serves as a Director on the boards of Qualcomm Corporation and the American Council on Germany. He also serves on the University of California President's Council on the National Laboratories.

ANNE-MARIE SLAUGHTER is Dean of the Woodrow Wilson School of Public and International Affairs at Princeton University. She is also President of the American Society of International Law. Prior to becoming Dean, she was the J. Sinclair Armstrong Professor of International, Foreign, and Comparative Law and Director of Graduate and International Legal Studies at Harvard Law School.

LAWRENCE H. SUMMERS is Co-chair of the Task Force and President of Harvard University. Dr. Summers has taught on the faculty at Harvard University and the Massachusetts Institute of Technology. He has served in a series of senior public policy positions, including Political Economist for the President's Council of Economic Advisers, Chief Economist of the World Bank, and Secretary of the Treasury of the United States. In 1993 he received the John Bates Clark Medal, given every two years to the most outstanding American economist under the age of forty.

DANIEL K. TARULLO is Professor of Law at Georgetown University Law Center. During the Clinton administration he was, successively, Assistant Secretary of State for Economic and Business Affairs, Deputy Assistant to the President for Economic Affairs, and Assistant to the President for International Economic Affairs.

LAURA D'ANDREA TYSON is on the Board of the Council on Foreign Relations. She is also Dean of London Business School. Dr. Tyson served the Clinton administration as the President's National Economic Adviser, and also as a member of the President's National Security Council and Domestic Policy Council. Prior to her appointment as National Economic Adviser, she served as Chairman of the White House Council of Economic Advisers.

Task Force Members

STEPHEN M. WALT* is Academic Dean at the John F. Kennedy School of Government at Harvard University, where he holds the Robert and Renee Belfer Professorship in International Affairs. He previously taught at Princeton University and the University of Chicago. Professor Walt is the author of *The Origins of Alliances* (1987) which received the Edgar S. Furniss National Security Book Award, and *Revolution and War* (1996), as well as numerous articles in international politics and foreign policy.

*The individual has endorsed the report and submitted an additional view.

TASK FORCE OBSERVERS

CAROLINE ATKINSON
Council on Foreign Relations

LEE FEINSTEIN
Council on Foreign Relations

BENN STEIL
Council on Foreign Relations

Selected Reports of Independent Task Forces Sponsored by the Council on Foreign Relations

†*Iraq: One Year After* (2004)
   Thomas R. Pickering and James R. Schlesinger, Co-Chairs; Eric P. Schwartz,
   Project Director
* †*Nonlethal Weapons and Capabilities* (2004)
   Graham T. Allison and Paul X. Kelly, Co-Chairs; Richard L. Garwin,
   Project Director
* †*New Priorities in South Asia: U.S. Policy Toward India, Pakistan, and Afghanistan*
   (2003)
   Frank G. Wisner II, Nicholas Platt, and Marshall M. Bouton, Co-Chairs;
   Dennis Kux and Mahnaz Ispahani, Project Co-Directors
* †*Finding America's Voice: A Strategy for Reinvigorating U.S. Public Diplomacy* (2003)
   Peter G. Peterson, Chair; Jennifer Sieg, Project Director
* †*Emergency Responders: Drastically Underfunded, Dangerously Unprepared* (2003)
   Warren B. Rudman, Chair; Richard A. Clarke, Senior Adviser; Jamie F. Metzl,
   Project Director
* †*Burma: Time for Change* (2003)
   Mathea Falco, Chair
* †*Meeting the North Korean Nuclear Challenge* (2003)
   Morton I. Abramowitz and James T. Laney, Co-Chairs; Eric Heginbotham,
   Project Director
* †*Chinese Military Power* (2003)
   Harold Brown, Chair; Joseph W. Prueher, Vice Chair; Adam Segal,
   Project Director
* †*Iraq: The Day After* (2003)
   Thomas R. Pickering and James R. Schlesinger, Co-Chairs; Eric P.
   Schwartz, Project Director
* †*Threats to Democracy* (2002)
   Madeleine K. Albright and Bronislaw Geremek, Co-Chairs; Morton H.
   Halperin, Project Director; Elizabeth Frawley Bagley, Associate Director
* †*America—Still Unprepared, Still in Danger* (2002)
   Gary Hart and Warren B. Rudman, Co-Chairs; Stephen Flynn, Project Director
* †*Terrorist Financing* (2002)
   Maurice R. Greenberg, Chair; William F. Wechsler and Lee S. Wolosky, Project
   Co-Directors
* †*Enhancing U.S. Leadership at the United Nations* (2002)
   David Dreier and Lee H. Hamilton, Co-Chairs; Lee Feinstein and Adrian
   Karatnycky, Project Co-Directors
* †*Testing North Korea: The Next Stage in U.S. and ROK Policy* (2001)
   Morton I. Abramowitz and James T. Laney, Co-Chairs; Robert A. Manning,
   Project Director
* †*The United States and Southeast Asia: A Policy Agenda for the New Administration*
   (2001)
   J. Robert Kerrey, Chair; Robert A. Manning, Project Director
* †*Strategic Energy Policy: Challenges for the 21st Century* (2001)
   Edward L. Morse, Chair; Amy Myers Jaffe, Project Director
* †*State Department Reform* (2001)
   Frank C. Carlucci, Chair; Ian J. Brzezinski, Project Coordinator;
   Cosponsored with the Center for Strategic and International Studies
* †*U.S.-Cuban Relations in the 21st Century: A Follow-on Report* (2001)
   Bernard W. Aronson and William D. Rogers, Co-Chairs; Julia Sweig and Walter
   Mead, Project Directors
* †*A Letter to the President and a Memorandum on U.S. Policy Toward Brazil* (2001)
   Stephen Robert, Chair; Kenneth Maxwell, Project Director
* †*Toward Greater Peace and Security in Colombia* (2000)
   Bob Graham and Brent Scowcroft, Co-Chairs; Michael Shifter, Project Director;
   Cosponsored with the Inter-American Dialogue
   †*Future Directions for U.S. Economic Policy Toward Japan* (2000)
   Laura D'Andrea Tyson, Chair; M. Diana Helweg Newton, Project Director

---

†Available on the Council on Foreign Relations website at www.cfr.org.
*Available from Brookings Institution Press. To order, call 800-275-1447.

www.ingramcontent.com/pod-product-compliance
Lightning Source LLC
Chambersburg PA
CBHW052108270326
41931CB00012B/2935

* 9 780876 093429 *